seventeen.

by Chelsey Junae Macklin

seventeen.

To anyone who ever loved me. Or tried their best.

To my motherhood.

To my father who kept telling me to publish this book.

To my family.

To the pain that I never thought would end.

To a never ending life of progression.

To the happy tears.

To Caleb, the love of my life for an eternity of eternities.

seventeen.

here is my heart that I have spilled on blank pages.

from young until now.

I hope my words fill you.

seventeen.

"Writing a book is hard. When I get the urge to write, most times I don't. When I actually do write, I feel proud and giddy because that feeling or thought I had resonated on paper. But then when I go back and read it again, I don't get the same deep feelings. It feels mediocre. And then I doubt everything. Why am I trying to write a book? I mean, I daydream about it all the time- about how the future will look but I have to get the material. I don't want to sound like anyone else, I don't want to feel like it's below average. There's something in me that wants all my original writing to not be edited because it allows for authenticity. But, if I don't get the same gut wrenching, powerful feeling as when I write it, I need to edit right?! I want to brand myself as a writer, be happy with what I read and keep the fun in the "business" simultaneously. I don't want writing to feel like a job and I want to be powerful and I want you to feel like you got stabbed in the heart with my words. Trying to find the balance, xox"

journal entry, 2017.

Nothing Lasts Forever

You know the saying, "Nothing lasts forever"? So many people say this and believe this. But with bitter intent. This love. This life. This relationship. This happiness. It ain't gonna last forever. Some people also use it as a cop out for making poor decisions. Burying friendships, relationships, disregarding people who still have time left in your life.

When I think about "nothing lasts forever", I agree. But not in a negative connotation. Hear me out. If everything lasted forever, why would life even be life? If you had your favorite flavor ice cream on a cone and every time you finished it, it refilled over and over again- same flavor, same taste, same everything, would you still love it the same? Nothing lasts forever because things lose value so they need to be redefined. Constantly. Whatever the "thing" may be. When it comes to love, REAL love does last forever but it will never be the same love. People change, circumstances change and honestly, things grow stale when you get used to them for too long unfortunately. Redefine your love, redefine yourself, redefine your surroundings. Life is about evolving. Nothing lasts forever because circumstances in life are constantly and simultaneously changing. So, when you say nothing lasts forever, you're right. It's time to change whatever you were used to so that thing can be TIMELESS. Something staying the same and lasting forever or something morphing from time to time for healthy growth to be TIMELESS. Longevity is important. So is change, even though some may not like it including myself. Nothing lasts forever you say? You're right... but grow up and think about it in the correct way. Perspective is everything in this world.

I feel like I'm going to be by myself forever. I feel like I'm always going to be doing this alone. I feel like I'm just not going to have a full family, even though me and Caleb are FULL enough. I feel like my nights will always be me sitting on the couch after the storm of my 2-year-old has settled. I feel like I'm always going to cry for no reason from being lonely but I will always feel strong because I do it alone. I feel like I'm always going to have to calculate how I'm going to get home with bags. How I'm gonna get home from the supermarket. The laundry mat. With a child by myself. I feel like I'm always going to be annoyed at my family and then when I don't wanna talk to them anymore, feel like I have no one left. I feel like I'm always going to have anxiety when I think about my future. Because I think my future will look the same as my past and present.

2/12/17, 12:08 AM

Thirteen.

people leaving was my worst fear
you asked me what my worst fear was
and I don't know if you were expecting me to say
spiders or snakes
but without hesitation
I said abandonment
Silence trickled the room, like rain drops slowly
falling down a window pane
watching them race and fall into each other
you probably don't even remember that moment
but I'll never forget it
Because where I end up now, it's like you conjured
together this sadistic plan all along
How do you tell someone you love them?
And plague them with their worst nightmare?
maybe the silence that night was trying to scream
to me
I'll really never forget that
because this was the horror movie of my life
And holding onto something that didn't want to be
held on to had my hand bleeding like a water fall
onto the floor
And whenever someone does the slightest thing...
my hand has calloused over
and when I try to hold on to something now,
I can't feel it
So I let it go.

seventeen.

I've never felt this unhappy in my entire life.

9/8/15
6:35 PM

Eclipse

Every single day before the 17th of July,
I wanted your hands to caress my back.
Now, I'm afraid that another set of hands
will be willing to touch me so deep
that I don't only feel his fingers just on my skin
...but I'll tell him to keep his hands to himself

Talk to Me

sometimes when the day is said and done,
I feel like it was trying to tell me something
some days it's clear, other days I can't see the signs
clearly
but I'm very in tune with God and the Universe
and our conversations can be lengthy

Wish

I wish I didn't doubt things
I wish I was a little shorter
I wish I could lose some of my stomach
I wish people would shut up sometimes
I wish I had an infinite amount of money
but then again I don't
I wish my grandmother was still alive
I wish Mark was still alive
I wish I didn't have to have this pain in my chest
when I'm mad, sad, or stressed
I wish I talked more
I wish people were more loyal
I wish people wouldn't judge without knowing
I wish things didn't go wrong
I wish I could take back falling in love at 16
I wish I didn't have an overactive mind
I wish I had more money
I wish I didn't worry so much
I wish people wouldn't be so stubborn, including
myself at times
I wish songs wouldn't remind me of certain things
I wish my hair was longer
I wish tears didn't exist
I wish my neighbors would stop making so much
noise while I'm writing
I wish I wasn't so nice at times
I wish people wouldn't say sorry and do the same
thing again
I wish more people were genuine

I wish I wasn't a sucker for love
I wish people wouldn't have to sleep in tunnels and
under bridges because they have nowhere else to
go
I wish I would've won best dressed in high school
I wish I could get kissed in the rain
I wish I could feel how much somebody loves me
just by the way they look at me
I wish the Knicks would've won tonight instead of
losing by 28
I wish I didn't have to wish
I wish my brother would've never got into so much
trouble
I wish I could take people's pain away
I wish I knew what people were thinking when
they're zoned out on the train
I wish I knew what people were thinking when they
stared at me
I wish I wasn't such a sweetheart
I wish I had closure
I wish my room was yellow
I wish I didn't have nightmares and weird dreams
I wish you didn't get that funny feeling when your
leg or foot falls asleep and tries to wake back up
I wish people would care more
I wish I was someone's #1
I really wish I didn't have to wish
I wish bad feelings didn't exist
I wish I could still use my favorite pen and the ink
never ran out
I wish people knew real love

I wish... that I didn't have to wish
But what I always say and what I live by- never
dwell on the things you can't change unless you
want to drive yourself absolutely crazy

I Can Only Dream

I want you to love me until I can't breathe, love me
until I turn blue
Immerse me, I wanna feel you take a breath when I
do
tell me you love me. and I wanna feel it in my soul
when we make love, I want your mother to feel it
in her womb like the kicks she used to feel when
she created you for me
kiss me and I want birds to sing a song that they
created from seeing us love each other
Love me when it hurts
Love me until it hurts
buy me flowers that smell like how my body leaks
for you at the touch of your finger tips
Make love to me like you never have before
get mad at the fact that you love me so much and
you can't explain it
Don't make any promises to me
Show me
show me like God shows us waterfalls and sunsets
and clear blue waters and the power of thunder
and lightning and the passion of a flooding rain
and every unique shaped cloud in the sky
and how the sun is always still there even when it's
cloudy

Kalief

Have you ever thought about the guilt I have as a
mother for bringing a black boy into a world that
hates him?
I feel guilty for making you out of love
and eating that green smoothie to make your brain
grow in my belly
Only for this hell hole to see you for your skin color
and not what's in your soul
just to watch you grow so harmoniously in love
with life
To grow up and see faces that look like you on the
news
and not because they saved a dog from a burning
building
I'm sorry
I wish I could save you from THIS burning building.
Have you ever imagined the guilt I have for
bringing you here?
sometimes a mother's arms aren't good enough as
a safe haven
You are Them and They are You.
And if I ever look at you and gently say, "I'm sorry",
please don't ask me what I'm apologizing for

Dedicated to Caleb Christopher.
Kalief Browder.
Venida Browder.

Power Trip

I'm sitting in a cab, surrounded by a late night
darkness
in my drunken bliss
The cab driver went the wrong way
but how could I be upset with Patron spilling
through my pores
we pull up to a red light
I'm not thinking about anything but kissing Caleb's
forehead when I get inside
Alongside me, I see a bus full of lights, sobering me
quickly
and the hospital I had been to maybe a year and
change earlier from today
all I asked was about a girl texting you goodnight in
the wee hours of the morning
As Caleb kicks and we lay across from each other,
the room reeks of distance and unspoken emotions
First being drunk with alcohol to being intoxicated
by memories, I never knew...
that sitting in that emergency room
because you punched the mirror out of anger
not only that your hand might be broken
but our relationship was broken too
you asked me why I didn't put my ring on as I
stupidly followed you to the hospital to see if you
were good
and instantly, I should've seen your need for
reassurance

Because you knew you would never be good
enough for me.
In hindsight, it's like Rome falling and nobody
seeing it coming
oblivious to the obvious
Powerless, punching a glass mirror was a desperate
need to take some power back
I had all the power all along and still do
And all you have is that scar on your knuckle

PTSD

It's the flashbacks that always get me
because it's not bitterness or rage that I feel
I'm content with knowing that my life is supposed
to be this way
Maybe resentment could be the word, I'm not
sure.
dirty diapers, when his favorite word is NO, those
days where you feel like you have nothing left but
you have to find the will to go on from somewhere
War.
many come back from war as different people
World War I, World War II
The war I fought has no name but it will go down in
history
and the constant reminder I get every day is that I
fought my hardest but still lost the fight
Guilt eats at me
"I should've known better"
"You probably saw red flags"
the small moment when I realized was probably
when you took the Moet bottle but not the brand
new baby bag
Stupid me, it took me that long to realize
War.
you never come back the same
Like how I slept on my couch for two months
straight with my baby on my chest because my
room reeked of you still

Or the sacred moments that turned to dust like
when you came to visit the next day when I had
him
And the night before when you told me you felt
complete
Did you purposely make yourself broken again?
I mean, it's all that you were used to in your life-
brokenness
Somehow I thought you could be glue
I used to have to strategize coming home- what
hand I was going to hold the stroller in, what arm
the groceries would be on, baby bag on my back
and oh yeah, the baby.
Groceries put away, sleeping baby after a bath to
wash away the day, get ready for the next day...
maybe eat?
All this to feel that little victory at night to do it all
again tomorrow
But then I get on the couch, the TV is on but it's
watching me
and the silence is so deafening, it makes you hear
him call you a bitch again as he walked down the
same hallway that you're now crying in
I used to reach for my ring on my finger a lot still
even though it wasn't there anymore
One time, I went in the closet, saw a shirt of yours
and got nauseous
The maternity picture of us in the living room has
been replaced with an enchanted garden full of
flowers
Caleb sometimes stared at the picture

I always wondered if he was still looking for us
it comes in waves.
and sometimes I wish the waves would wash me
away with them
the darkness can consume me if I let it
Like puppet strings on my back, you think you'll
always have that grasp
sometimes I ask myself, will you?
War.
glass shattering, loud voices
the pregnancy test we bought had two tests- one
still in the cabinet, the other in my drawer which
was Caleb
a weird, sentimental keepsake
My uncle was an army vet and my dad said when
he came back,
he was never the same
I mean, imagine seeing explosions
and being alone
and fighting for a "greater good"
but seeing things die
Even after years, when you're sitting in your living
room
in your favorite chair
all the memories come crashing at once
and you start to shake
and you smell the same smells
and hear the same voices, feel the same feelings
and your tongue gets dry
and suddenly you remember that they were all
memories but your mind played a trick on you

seventeen.

The war I fought will never have a name
but I'll always feel like I lost

"How Could You?"

I'm sitting here with swollen eyes
and my shoulder has a sharp pain
and I feel like a failure
My lip is quivering in self doubt
and all I want is my baby
How could I do this? I'm just about to burst with
regret like a balloon filled to capacity
anybody who ever reads this or if they knew I felt
this way would probably shout,
"Oh, stop. You're a great mom."
"You take such good care of your baby."
I agree.
But I teeter back and forth between the line that
separates
"My biggest blessing wouldn't be here if I wasn't
living my worst nightmare"
and
"I should've saw this before sowing seeds in rotten
dirt."

Faucet

You have the power to break me
and I'm giving you that
You have the power to shatter me
and I'm giving you that
You have the power to send me into a never
ending spiral
and I'm giving you that
but you also have the power to propel me into
another dimension with your tenderness
with your longing eyes looking into mine
with ego-free love
falling to your knees at any chance you get to
worship me, your Goddess
please choose wisely
the pain of losing me is something you will never
be ready for
just ask anyone before you
they have the shivers, the shakes- strung out
on the love I gave freely
like running water

Monsters

am I allowed to dance with the monsters in my
head or should I let them sing their own song?
I mean, they're ugly and nasty and dirty and no
good for me
But for some reason, I always wanna waltz in the
mud with them
nobody ever sees our moon lit dance around my
mind
but we always hold each other close
I have grit and grime all over me
nobody ever sees our moon lit dance
but sometimes I feel like people can see the muck
on my skin
like, sometimes I just know that they see my eyes
cross into each other
and how ugly I get on the inside
transcends to the outside
I know people see it
I reek of sadness because of dancing with the
monsters in my head
I try to hide our samba. they never really go away.
I know our moon lit dance in the mud can't be
good for me but I do it anyway
...beaming in all white and brightness, can I dance
with an angel for once?

Letter to Chelsey

I have to forgive you for being so hard on yourself
I have to forgive you for all the self-pity
I have to forgive you for crying until it feels like
your chest is going to cave in
I have to forgive you for never forgiving yourself
I have to forgive you for living in the moment and
not thinking long term
I have to forgive you for not always seeing who you
really were this whole time
I have to forgive you for thinking yourself into
migraines
I have to forgive you for stressing your heart when
you know you can handle anything
I have to forgive you for falling for the sweet
nothings in your ear, even when you thought you
had heard them all
I have to forgive you for yelling at your son out of
times of frustration
but you do always tell him you're sorry.
I have to forgive you for holding your mistakes on
your back longer than you need to
I have to forgive you for abusing your body,
physically and emotionally
I have to forgive you for feeling guilty when you
don't wash the dishes or clean and go to bed
instead
I have to forgive you for not being able to write
during a block

I have to forgive you for misunderstanding yourself
and other people
I have to forgive you for being hurt and having to
decipher if someone is being real or fake
I have to forgive you for feeling like a bad mom
I have to forgive you for drinking Hennessy to
drown your thoughts
I have to forgive you for just now realizing that this
is all a process
I have to forgive you for never forgiving yourself

Soul Tie

Every edge of your body fits
perfectly into mine
We made a puzzle we never knew existed
We made a rhythm with our bodies that made the
room sing
you made me sing
sing your song, over and over
You knew my body, almost as good as I knew it
myself
we connected every dot, crossed every T, bridged
every gap
you taught me to see myself how you saw me and
I'm forever thankful.
In the likeness of Gods.
every time you made me arch my back, I felt more
like a woman every single time
we melted into each other
my body craved you like water
I needed you and how you made me feel wrapped
with a bow and given to me like a gift every single
time
When it's over, how do I get rid of the shivers
craving you?
how do I tell the goosebumps on my skin to go
away when I need you?
my whole body shakes and I drip with honey when
I think of you
But I'm also sweating bullets, trying to rid the
toxins you left behind

if we enter each other's space again, it will always
be beautiful
but the thing is that it never stays that way
Let my soul detox you away
and find new ways to feed itself
I'll always remember you

Free Yourself

my skin is bleeding
a bright, blood red that will hurt your eyes
and make your breathing heavy
they told me I had to rip myself
completely open to feel better
so that's what I'm doing
and it's not just hearsay- I feel it in my spirit to do
so...
so here I go
slowly dissecting the vessel that stores my soul, it
hurts so good
my bones are exposed with a dull white that
reflects brokenness
my heart is still intact, though beating rather slowly
my insides are heaving up and down like they've
been holding secrets. hurt. anger.
the blood is pouring like a faucet onto the floor but
I keep cutting
it hurts but it has to be done
insecurity, doubt, loneliness, anger, confusion
they all spill into my hands
and I throw them to the side
the tumors that are killing me can no longer stay
I have to rip myself apart
there's so much blood, my mind and the floor look
like Halloween
am I killing myself?
keep digging, keep cutting, keep going
rip yourself completely open

there are parts of you that is sewage- none of it can
stay
rip yourself completely open and free your
consciousness from its own prison
its own holding cell
my eyes are googly, not focused
I have to readjust them to look straight
no wonder I always feel like I'm moving backwards
my mouth has been sewn shut with the fear of
what other's think being the stitching that forbids
my words
I carefully open the stitches and
unsaid feelings spew out like a projectile vomit
the words are rotten but I read them despite their
smell
and keep them in my memory
my brain is glowing, beaming. I leave that as it is
But the poisonous thoughts
unwanted self-destruction
self-reflection
cancerous repetitive actions
evil, unwanted sabotage
I am a wreck but a beautiful one
like a surgeon of my own destiny, I rip myself apart
for good cause
release, renew, replenish, restock, detox
and stitch myself back up
don't ever wait for anybody else to free you
free yourself.

Laying Next to Me

I love how you never have an odor
you always smell like love
I love how you melt into my hands when I touch
you
Like an M&M that's been in the bag too long
you smell like peace
smiling into the shadows of the room,
I really don't feel like this is real life
it's scary, I know
but you were never afraid of the dark
love with everything you have
and even though no human on this earth really
knows how to do that,
do the closest thing to that- love entirely.
vulnerability is your Achilles heel
like pancakes on a Sunday morning,
the ridged edges always end up showing the light
and fluffy inside
let it go
it's scary but let everything go
love is not only a drug
but a kryptonite
a dead end- or what seems like
keep going with your heart always swelling out of
your chest
it's gonna hurt sometimes but that's alright
what's life without a little punch where its sore
I love you. forever. please let me love you forever.

Rules of Engagement

I'm thankful for the complexity of life
every corner you turn, you don't know
if it's a miracle or a monster
but even the monsters shine light
I don't have the greatest life
Or do I?
but I say that to express that I appreciate storms
and turmoil
too many people let the black hole that we call this
world make them weary
absolutely lost in the Bermuda Triangle of the mess
and never come back
weariness is warranted, we don't live in any sort of
paradise
but we let the cloudiness be the only thing in our
tunnel vision and that's where we fail miserably
appreciate sunsets and rainbows
laugh while you cry
crying is cleansing
smile at random people
dance down the street
be in darkness but don't get consumed
it will all pass
your mind is as strong as you want it to be. mind
over matter is not a myth.
And being happy isn't either
when everything is constantly raining on your
parade, strap on your boots
and walk through it with your trumpet

live in love
love will get you through
love is the most powerful thing on this planet- if we
know it correctly.
radiate peace, walk through life knowing you have
an abundance at all times
even if that abundance is something you can't
physically touch
these tall buildings, these corrupt people, diseased
minds, the stench of badness you smell in the air
in the clouds is something more powerful than the
most mentally distorted person or thing there is
make sure you live
and live knowing your mind either creates your
worst nightmare
or the closest thing to a fairytale that this tainted
world can offer

Warmth

look how you got his whole existence drizzling
through your fingers
like melted caramel oozing into the pot slowly
trust your gut
because you got it like they say you do
you just never believe it when they say it
I'm the queen of everything I touch
now drift off to your second dream
and I'll tip toe my hands on the top of your skin
and send you straight to your third
I have the power to blow you away like dust in the
palm of my hand
or keep you like a bad habit that I will never shake
what's the old saying?
"forever is a long time"
"nothing lasts forever"
How about we do it for the long haul?

A Drunk Mind.

i fucjin hare you porce of fukin shot. who do tou
think tou are dumd fuck. you left me to tmdo
wveryrhign by myself and you think ingive a fuck
about you. idc if you live on the d traib nogga food
for you. rhis id not supposed to be mmy life and I
blamw you. just wantvsinethbody to love me and
take care of ne. i fan do it by myself but I dint want
to. im drunk abd i wish i was hone with you fuvkinf
vecause caleb finally went to slepp. Ilovebyoiu and
you shoukdnt ve with anybody hut me bc i know yo
love u and take car of you. i hate you, go away
forever please. npbody asked for this and i hate
you for making this my life. youre aupposed to be
here

Footie Pajamas

have you ever held your baby as they slept?
the weight of their world is all on you
the only care they have is readjusting themselves
to get comfortable against your warm body
listening to your heart beat as the lullaby they've
always known
their limp body relying on your care at all times
holding their fragile body with one hand
and their head full of soft hair with the next, with
that smell that only babies have
if you put them down, it's the biggest betrayal but
they won't remember it in the morning
but they will wake up looking for you with yearning
eyes and panic
because you're not there
until you get to them and they reassure you with a
smile
there you are- my safe place
imagine a tiny little creature having that much trust
and love in you?
the purest form.
It's what makes the world go round
and really the only thing left that keeps my heart
beating
even when they outgrow their footie pajamas,
you'll never outgrow that feeling of unconditional
love and acceptance

Half on a Baby

my mother has always been warm but had ice
running through her veins
it wasn't her fault
my dad has always been the manly man with a
heart made of everything soft and plushy
explosions can happen here
many of them have
some days I see my mom in my reflection
but most days my heart looks like my dad
I see my mother in my shadow while walking
when stubbornness is worn like a shield in a battle
that I made up in my mind
my dad always appears in the depths
when I'm thinking and when I feel like nobody
understands me
or when I smile at you but inside,
something in me is pleading for help
I try to detach my parents from myself as much as
possible
so that when I catch my reflection walking past a
store window,
I don't see failed words spilling from my mouth
or I don't see sensitivity making my flesh peel,
making me seem weaker
I wanna see me- whoever that might be today.
But motherhood has caused me to try on my
mother's old battle gear

and having my heart ripped out of my chest
repeatedly, I wear my dad's sensitivity like a badge
of honor that I try to hide
mommy and daddy would battle sometimes
one day- passive like knowing there's an elephant
in the room but ignoring it
and the next day- an all-out sword fight.
because I am a product of them both,
I fight myself a lot I think
fire and ice
wet and dry
passive aggressive and passionate
nonchalant and fiery
and low and high
the depths of me will always be mine entirely
but I hear whispers of my parents in my ears all the
time
I speak to my son and lose my breath when I hear
Gyda's voice come from my own mouth
somebody pushes me on the train
and the Charles in me begs me to relax
but I feel my fingers clenching into each other,
making a fist at the same time
She tells me that I'm good by myself
He tells me to love and be myself no matter what-
but protect your peace always
my DNA is wired with the likeness of you two.
because I am the both of you in one flesh, I am
always at war with myself
but somehow, being on each side of the spectrum
helps my perspective

I love my mother.
I love my father.
I love myself.
every tangled part of me is just Him and Her
pushing each other back and forth
hoping to show in the eyes of what they created,
which is me
even my body betrays me when it can't choose if it
wants my mother's big, sparkly eyes first
or my dad's dry skin on a winter day
or when my mother and I have the same pimple or
blemish on our face in the same exact spot always
and our twin birth marks on the back of our hands
I'm 100% me but I look like a perfect 50/50 split of
my mother and father
Inside and out

Wait for It

Men have always loved me
loved me like they knew how
and me being me, I accept it in its raw and natural
form
without complaints
I've had relationships where I've felt loved
But maybe not completely
But I accepted their offering to my altar
men have always loved me
but when things get cloudy, I start to see the storm
that they really are

Brownie

when I think about you,
I think about amber and vanilla scents
and how they make me feel calm and warm
when I think about you, I wanna listen to
Stay by Jodeci
We are One by Frankie Beverly
Love Ballad
Let's Stay Together by Al Green
you make me feel like R&B, the 90s way
you make me feel like a fall day
When I think about you,
I feel like true love
I feel like dissolving into you and never separating
When I think about you,
It makes everything okay and it makes the absence
of a few of my heart strings seem worth it
you make me feel like I never want to leave
like everything and nothing exists
I'll stay forever I promise- just keep making me feel
like hot chocolate
making me want to dive into your being every time
I swim and always find a new treasure I wanna
keep
You make me feel like a deep breath before a big
speech
But also a deep breath when I sit on my couch after
a long day
the highest high and a great mellow
When I think about you,

I just wanna be yours
at your surrender whenever you say so
can I just ask you to keep making me feel this way?
I just feel like I can't go without it

Abandonment Issues

please don't.
I know this time it's partly my fault but please
don't.
You're not like everybody else
but for you to be on the opposite side of the
spectrum
and still try to leave me,
please don't.
I will have no hope left in me
if you leave, that's the end of me
I made a mistake living life figuring you would
always be there
I can be wrong too.
I'm just tryna find my way
please don't
I don't even like saying the word
please don't... leave.
Without you, there won't be a me
my heart keeps exploding into my stomach when I
think about the things you said
I feel guilt but then I feel sorry
Sorry that for once, I did what I thought was best
for me
but also shattered you
you've been through hell and I never intended to
keep you there
but please don't
you've been through worse and I know I sound
selfish- I've hurt you

but I promise I can love you better
please don't leave me

Instagram Post

sometimes I still can't believe I even have you. sometimes I feel like I'm not enough for you. am I doing this right, am I doing that right? every day when I wake up, I see your face and every night when I go to bed, I watch you sleep. nothing in this world can compare to that feeling of happiness. you're a grown man now, you're the big 1-year-old and you've already taught me more than you will ever know. this past year with you has been some sort of magic and sometimes idk how I do it but you help me to do this every day and make motherhood a hobby that I love. let's keep growing in love together. I'm excited to spend forever with you. I love you with everything in my soul Caleb Christopher.

The day I've been waiting for and expecting... but just not this way. So, I walk in the house at 2:10 AM. The day was cool. Anyway, I get in the house and lock the door. My brother is in my parent's room and, as soon as he hears me come in, he storms out of their room. Drunk face but red eyes so it was a crying face too. I walk in my parent's room innocently. They say he was asking where I was and talking about how they treat me differently. Annoyed, I changed the subject and ask my mom to come in my room. It's anniversary time for them so I just wanted to show her the things I bought for my dad. So, I unzip my coat, lay it on my bed and start to open the Yankee Store bag with my dad's gifts in it. My mom soon trails in behind me to my room, stands beside me and says, "So, your brother thinks you're having sex. Are you?" The look on her face was waiting for my answer. A worried, concerned look- bracing herself for what she was about to hear. My body froze then instantly relaxed as I shook my head yes. Tears start to well up in my mother's eyes and she hugs me tight. But it's not a regular hug. She hugs me tight with both arms then strokes my hair with her left hand as if she wanted to say, "...my baby". At first, I'm not crying but it's only a certain amount of time that I can see as well as hear my mom sob until I burst into tears as well. I sit down on my bed, tell her to sit down too and we have THE CONVERSATION. The one you see on TV where the mother and daughter talk about IT. That conversation. What do I feel at this point? Relieved, anxious, guilty, but loved. The way she spoke to me was exactly how I wanted and needed to hear what she had to say. Which made me feel guiltier because my mother felt that I would've come to her and tell her myself and I should've. But she understood that I didn't have any idea how to go about the situation. She never had to tell her mom- she just knew. She asked me if I loved him and if he loved me. How I had decisions to make which I knew way before she told me that. What hurt me bad was when she said my brother said I was having sex and she said if I was that I would've told her. When she said that, my brother said, "Yeah, iight. Okay." Which was very inconsiderate because I would never want to make my mother feel that she's not approachable even though she's really not. I'm the only girl. She had never gone through the situation and I had no idea how she would take it. And I'm the type of person to keep all my problems, burdens, and anxieties to myself and deal with them by myself. I hate feeling like I'm imposing my feelings or problems on others, especially those I love. Like my mother. I don't want her to worry about me. She has a million and one other things to worry about. I felt that I could handle myself. What I don't understand is why my brother basically sold me out like that. I understand that it was the liquor but that has to stop too. Because now I have a certain animosity towards my brother. I know it won't last but still. It could've been avoided if we only had an adult conversation about things. He's just been different lately but I just wish he would understand that everybody is not against him. I'm always on my brother's side.

After I had that conversation with mommy, I didn't want her to leave me. So, I took my boots off and she laid down with me. She wrapped the blanket around me like when I was little and I laid there and cried some more and she caressed my back and flipped through channels. Ironically, The Women was on. Today, my mother realized that I was a woman. I have so many other things to experience but I am a woman. After a while of flipping through channels, she left me and said, "I'm going to bed. Love you." But what made me feel better is that, even though it's weird is, "I'm not waking you up in the morning. Wake yourself up." It was regular mommy. The mother I knew all these years was still there after what she just found out. Of course she probably went in her bed and cried herself to sleep because I did the exact same thing but I just thanked her out loud to myself for being herself. And that's how it happened.

12/9/12
5:26 PM

Ground Rules

pray more
cut unnecessary spending
maintain regular cleaning habits- physically and
spiritually
grow hair bigger
text him with a peaceful heart
let everything go
do not stress anything out of your control
think positive and focus on the happy thoughts
spend as much time with Caleb as possible
indulge in work/focus
less social media. put your phone down.

Mosaic Glass

the sadness is filling my body like air fills a balloon
I feel like if I have one more thought,
I'm going to explode
Do you know what this feels like?
if I actually burst, there would be nothing left
idk what I'm supposed to give anybody
that may eventually come along
but I'll give them all of the nothingness I have left
nobody deserves to live with a broken heart
and nobody who wants to mend it should be given
broken pieces

I Last Forever

taste me and see if I'm the flavor you crave
even if you don't keep me forever,
you'll never forget the honey that drips from your
lips

Self Care Tactics

Always remember the "I" in "We"
I've lost myself many times forgetting this

Intuition

don't ask questions that
your gut already told you the answer to

Sprout

sometimes I have to remind myself that it's okay to
get a drink
and sit in the corner of your living room on the
floor and cry
and not be okay
and you don't have to know why you're not okay
there's always a root to an emotion
and even if you don't know what the root is,
plant the tree and see how it's leaves grow

seventeen.

Scent and Chill

I still smell you on me hours after you leave
How can I not want you to be mine?
all mine
don't give me a puzzle piece
and another person has the others
because if we ever cross paths,
and connect the portions you gave us
we'll see the full picture you never wanted any of
us to see

Unicorn

obsessed with smelling good,
tasting good,
and getting whatever I want and need
on my own

Purpose

when you look at your child,
just stare.
for a few seconds, a couple minutes, even hours
just stare at your child and all you will see is life
and all the beauty that sprouts from it
I looked at my son
and I felt roses start blossoming in my chest.
stare at your child
you'll learn everything you will ever need to know
about why you're here at this very moment

I don't really know what it's going to take for me to see love as something "good" again. I don't even know how I feel towards marriage any more, I just feel like everyone will end up leaving after a while. It's like having PTSD. Especially since "perfection" burst into flames so quickly for me. I don't want to become a product of my environment. Especially being a black woman, I want to keep my softness but it's difficult when people make you have to create this shell. Then, after being emotionally beaten over and over, there comes the callous. I don't really feel anything anymore, only when it comes to Caleb. Anything else, I don't really care about.

Sometimes I find myself trying to define what I feel, what I am, and what I want and right now, I'm in a state of limbo but it feels like I need to be here right now. All those who wander aren't lost. Even though at times it's frustrating, being the structured person that I am.

I have so much inside of me and sometimes I feel stuck and idk how to get it out or what to say or what to do. But I have so much to say, to write. So many things I wanna do. I'm not sure what this block is but I'm trying to get rid of it. I feel like I'm wasting potential.

6/16/17
10:26 PM

Goldie

"Ehh, I'm alright. But how are you?"
the most unselfish person I've ever known
and ever will know
and we didn't deserve you
sometimes I feel like you're gone because of that
reason
we gotta feel what it's like not to have
something that we never should have had in the
first place
nobody knows the pain you felt or
the thoughts you had everyday
but I swear I will never forget your laugh
I hear it randomly sometimes when I think about
you
I get a warm feeling knowing that you're resting
Maybe that's what you needed
and this was the only way
but Security is still roaming Pascual's store
aimlessly, talking about LeBron
I try to get the boys to still talk to each other
because I know that would make you happy
every other thing that happens to Trav on the daily
reminds him of you
there's always a story to tell
you were 1 of 1.
some days I go about life and I'll feel okay
but there's something off
something missing
and it's you

But I'm trying my hardest to do the right thing so I
can see you again
as soon as I heard you were gone, that's all I
thought about
I think when people pass away,
Everybody should leave an impact like you did but
they won't Goldie
here's to the nights we were all drunk
and you falling asleep but swearing you were
awake
here's to the days I thought about you randomly
and decided to check on you to see how you were
I know you weren't "fine" and I know you weren't
"okay".
But I took your word for it and waited until the
next time I had to check on my brother
just rest... please
you deserve it
We miss you but we're "alright" out here
For once, let us take on your pain and your burdens
because you always took ours as your own.
We're "fine".
We're "okay".
Forever Goldie.

Dedicated to Mark Anthony Stevenson and Travis
Darnel Coley, forever my brother's keepers

Give

I just feel like I'm the one always
doing the saving
but who's gonna save me?
Why can't I be the one breaking down?
because when I'm trying to get
you through your storm,
I'm fighting rain too

Guilty Pleasures

eating ice
the feel of a new pen in my hand
seeing Caleb happy
a good book
loving someone
those train rides where you almost miss your stop
because you're recapping your whole life in your
mind from 125th to 59th Street
picking the nail color at the salon
moisturizing and twisting my hair
the color yellow
loving someone
someone loving me back
brisk fall nights where I have to wear a jacket and
leaves are everywhere
when my parents wear matching Adidas suits
talking to my brother on the phone everyday
when I have an outfit that I look cute in
when someone I love looks at me and my whole
body blushes
being drunk with people I love
coconut oil, shea butter, black soap, my rose water
witch hazel
moisturizing my body and smelling good
feeling good nostalgia
remembering a bad memory but taking good away
from it
when strangers smile at me and I smile back
a clean house

candles that smell like vanilla and smell like fall
knowing I have nothing to worry about
when Caleb is with Grammy and Pee Pah
natural hair tutorials
when people tell me how they feel about me
eating a chopped cheese after a night out
hearing Caleb talk and develop his tiny voice
laughing
somebody understanding- and listening to my
point of view although not necessarily agreeing
being held
caressing the lower of my back
falling asleep rubbing a warm body
laying in the dark and not saying anything
watching documentaries
that fuzzy feeling when you think about someone
you love
a good sleep, a good cry, street fairs
having someone remember something you told
them that you didn't think they would remember
going to Whole Foods, Trader Joe's, and random
spiritual shops
random epiphanies
learning something new about myself
when it's sunny but cool outside
nature. wine- moms love wine
when the Universe communicates and tells me
things
seeing or feeling something that makes me want to
write
watching Grey's Anatomy

seventeen.

watching the Science Channel
when someone admits they're wrong
because I never have a problem doing that
seeing light in someone's eyes
also seeing darkness so I can bring light
thinking, figuring things out
pomegranate seeds
Magnolia's red velvet cupcakes
The Alchemist by Paulo Coelho
Between the World and Me by Ta Nehisi-Coates
The Autobiography of Assata Shakur
being cold and wearing oversized clothes
being completely under a comfortable blanket
when I feed Caleb something healthy
Maya Angelou
Audrey Hepburn
shaving, being clean
loving until it hurts
being me and finding out who
that is every now and then

I've come to realize that I have this weird thing with control. I feel like it started because of certain events that have happened in the past and the fact that I don't trust anyone.

I know I am mostly reasonable with how I feel sometimes because I'm entitled to feel that way. But sometimes I have to let go and it scares me a little. Putting full trust in someone is hard but I'm doing it. That's another thing. I hate feeling vulnerable. I don't like the feeling that someone is capable of hurting me because it happened so many times before. I don't wanna feel that. Maybe that's why I'm always so on guard. I have to keep reminding myself that I have to believe in love and trust but not live in a fairytale either. I just have to find the balance, just like in everything else. Nobody ever knows what's going to happen. So I have to let go. I have to keep loving. Kissing him for no reason. Giving him my natural self. Giving him my all at all times. And not only for him but myself. It's a process and I give myself credit for handling these situations of self-reflection maturely and rationally. All I do is try.

8/29/13
1:33 PM

Hope

I've had writer's block for so long
Every time I write, something motivates me
whether it be love, anger, happiness
lately, I don't feel any specific feeling
I'm numb
maybe that's why my hand can't pick up my pen

I have to see another woman pull up to my home in her car with MY child... and the man who put a ring on my finger, only to take it back and leave me with this. and I'm supposed to just be okay.

3/25/17
2:32 PM

Wasted

There are so many nights when
I want to drown myself in liquor
But the trickle of thoughts pouring
Into the cup of my brain is brutal intoxication
enough

People really have no idea what I go through. The emotions, the pain, the anxiety, the hurt, loneliness. Just everything. Sitting in the park with my baby, right in front of Yankee Stadium and the only thing I'm thinking about is disappearing with him and nobody else. I don't wanna deal with anybody's stress, anybody's anger, anybody's overwhelming personality. He's sitting in his stroller dancing to the sound of the train coming into the station and that's really all the happiness I need.

8/24/16

As a writer, idk what it means for me to see a blank page and still be excited but have nothing to say, even with so much going on. I feel like I'm so deep in my head these days but I need to write. Lately, I've been feeling like I want to write a poetry book but I need the patience to do that. And write more. Write every day. Whenever I have a thought. I don't even just want it to be a poetry book- I want it to be something nobody has really ever done before. Original and only done by me. Raw, vulnerable. I'm gonna carry my book around with me. Maybe it'll help me get through some days. And praying more.

There's a lot that's been happening and there's been a lot that I've been feeling. I have to learn to write through it all. Through the pain, through the anxiousness, through everything. I want to look back at my writing and FEEL it. And if I'm going to write this book, I NEED other people to feel it too. Or as closely as possible.

Sometimes I just wonder what he's thinking. What he's REALLY going through. Not the front he puts on. And it's not a caring thing. I just want/need him to be humbled. Because he's not... even after all of this. I know he's hurting but I hope he's hurting enough. I can't see myself going through this for 18 years. I mean, once my baby can communicate, etc. it'll be much easier. But, even though, something has to give. And I keep praying because idk what that something is but Jehovah knows definitely. I just need him to fix it.

I don't deserve to live this life this way. And I'm not saying it's a bad life. But I deserve to be happier. Sometimes I feel selfish for even thinking that way because Caleb should be more than enough to make anyone happy. And he is enough and does absolutely make me happy. But to be walking down the block with bags, my baby and a stroller trying to figure out how I'm gonna get up the stairs? To have random moments of sadness because I feel like I failed my son? Even though it's not my fault? To wonder what I'm gonna tell my baby when he gets older? To crave a helping hand and a warm body when my baby goes to sleep and I'm sitting on the couch exhausted and alone? To be called "selfish" when everything I do is selfless? To have given somebody everything and ended up with nothing? To have to listen to somebody who has no idea what I go through every day and I have to go by whatever they say? To get anxious when I see the name of someone who was once my everything pop up on my phone? To have a ring on my finger the same time last year and now everything is long gone because I was sold a dream?

I really try not to think this way and blame myself. But it is my fault. I should have known. That's just what happens when you fall in love with somebody's potential and not who they really are. I'll have the life I want and need one day.

8/21/16
11:41 PM

Random

People hurt you exactly when they're supposed to
That's something higher than you clearing the path
of destruction
you think it hurts because they hurt you?
Because they left?
the healing will feel like cold butter on a scar
If they would've stayed, the scar would have you
on the floor
bleeding to death
and there would be no way to stop it

Love is Light

love is the sunrise
quiet but powerfully filling a dark room with light
slowly creeping like a thief
ready to steal the imperfections of the room,
realizing that the light made them perfect without
changing a thing
beaming- its energy both good and bad
misinterpreting its power because of its scary
greatness
love can be a sunset too
slowly bringing back the coldness you thought you
got rid of
you feel the brisk air giving you goosebumps as the
sun descends
it takes the brightness to somewhere else
besides in you
whether east or west,
the sun binds us
 we need it and in order for it to survive, it needs us
to continue to be needy
sunrise or sunset
love will always be brightness coming to
and fro.

Metamorphosis

while she's turning you into something else
something different
something you don't like
you're doing the same thing to me

It's All About You

Stop beating yourself up. It's literally killing you and making your body betray you. Speak up for yourself. Don't hold back. The more you hold in and keep to yourself, the sicker you will be. Physically and mentally. Just be free without thinking about what someone else will think. Be true to yourself. BE FREE. And you can only control yourself so just let go. Let it all go. Your health and future depend on it.

Stuck

anxiety is
feeling overwhelmed with every
big thing and every small thing
then having random moments of clarity
like, what am I even worried about?
the switch goes on and off in your brain
and it can be on and off at the same time
it's a weird life

The Creative

the creative gets more recognition than
the mathematician, for me
a creator is not calculated with robotic behavior,
learning and repeating
a systematic law of a certain thing
a creator is one color one day, and another color
the next
paving their own path of smartness
and learning how to change the world
without conformity

He knows what I want but last night, I told him I wanted to spend the rest of my life with him. I had the same feeling when I told him I loved him. You don't just say these things often and to anybody. I can't see my life any other way and I know nothing in life is promised but he was made for me and that's what I feel every time I see him. Even when we have our little moments. I'm not going to say I need him because I never feel like I need anybody and never will but the fact of the matter is, I don't want it any other way. I never believed in everything happening for a reason until I met him. I feel like this is destiny. Fate. The cards fell just as they were supposed to. Job interview this week and I wish it was Thursday already. I want to get my life moving with my everything. It's so close, I can taste it.

7/28/14
10:04 AM

Grit

I never knew I would feel
The strength God gave black women
To live in this imperfect world
I never knew I would know it so well
but now I know all about the bittersweet taste

NWTS

I'm not the same and I know in life,
you're supposed to evolve and grow
and learn
but I never wanted to be and feel and
think this way because no matter how
much change we ourselves go through,
our souls always remain true
the bitterness I feel is blinding to who I
really am and for right now, I'll ride the wave
I still see glimpses of her at times
the old me
I think that's how I see the difference
and I know she's still there

The Only One

the sunken feeling in my chest
when I think about not being the only one
depreciated in value, I start to lose my glow
choose yourself first

Black Hole

he has a million feelings
but no soul
imagine walking around
like a zombie
knowing how you feel
but with no guidance from the voice within
because there isn't one
there's no voice
no conscience
no good or bad
only walking in survival like it's your yellow brick
road
it cannot be
I cannot support
I will not
I cannot
You will devour me too
I already have bite marks on the side of
my face
and my blood is starting to feel like it has ice cubes
in it
look what you did
a human with no soul

Docket Number

nobody wants to look at each other
because we probably have the same sadness
and we don't wanna see it in each other's eyes
the air smells like file cabinets, sheets of paper, the
ink of pens, and worry
it feels like jail
if you don't do the right thing here, you might
really get there
gavels shatter the air as someone who barely even
knows your names decides the fate of your
children and your life
seems pretty "fair"
your social security number, where you were born,
your address- who does the child live with?
does the child need an attorney?
what color is the respondent's eyes?
How much money do you make?
Can you explain to me how you're the "good" one?
Can I have your soul please?!
I mean, what color underwear do I have on today,
too?
we might as well be at a candle lit dinner
but just handcuffed to the table
But the biggest question of all: how can I
manipulate you, the one in the black coat, who
knows nothing about my life, that I am the "fit"
individual?
seeing people's faces all day long and
flipping them like pages in a book and

forgetting the words as soon as you turn it
you don't know me, you don't know him, you don't
know my child, you don't know my life, you don't
know anything but the words that come out of our
mouths
the things we say to you are the candy
that we dangle in front of a baby, hoping you take
the bait and come to our side
you're oblivious to anything going on
but yet, the fate I will have to live is in the palm of
your hand
This system was put into place for a good cause
and sometimes good does come out of it
I just have a terrible problem with authority
Especially when you think you can take authority
over my life
and my child
and how I HAVE to live
and where I HAVE to drop my kid off
and WHEN I can communicate with him
and HOW I have to interact with a person
who doesn't seem to respect me in the least bit
"it's in the best interest of the child"
I know there are plenty of "mother's" who
come in here with flip flops flopping
and bonnet still on, probably didn't brush their
teeth
but popping their gum... who don't really know or
have the best interests of their child in mind
that's not me- I'm a protector and I don't need you
for anything

but in this building, we're all just identified as a
sheet of paper
with a docket number
I have a terrible problem with authority

A ring on my finger. A good job. A baby boy growing inside of me. A home to call my own. All of this happened and I'm actually still in shock. It's everything I ever wanted. To know that I have this beautiful little boy growing inside of me makes me more excited than I've ever been in my life but also nervous. I just want to do what's in his best interest. Eat the best things, give him ice cream that he loves every once in a while. I want him to get here as healthy as the most perfect baby that I'm imagining in my head. Another important thing is giving him good emotions to feed off of. I want him to be a happy baby and I don't think I've been giving him the best vibes to feel as he's growing because of what I've been going through. And no matter what, I need to fix that. I can't be selfish and I know my emotions get the best of me but what I can try to control to the best of my abilities, I should. No matter what. It's time to focus on him because that's where my thoughts and my life lives from now on, starting as soon as I found out he existed.

I have everything I've said I've wanted and I'm thankful. Being pregnant isn't easy and I knew it wouldn't be. But I can handle throwing up and being tired. But, as a person who is always in control of her emotions, the emotional struggle that I'm experiencing seems unbearable sometimes but it completely is. As a woman, I know it is and all I need is the support and will power to accept change and to be vulnerable in a way I've never been before.

Sometimes I just need the understanding that I'm going through a lot and I want the man of my life to be exactly that... a man. THE man. The one I need when I have nothing left. To pick me up when I'm beyond down. To put me first before anything. To console me when I'm crying. To be emotionally, spiritually, mentally attached to me. I'm carrying the next generation of you inside of me. To make me feel like the most precious thing in the world to him. To make me feel like everything will always be okay. To put pride aside and always make sure we're okay as a unit. I guess it's just because in 3 months, I won't be pregnant anymore and I don't wanna be discouraged or resentful to what I look back and see. It's difficult but I'm still here.

4/11/15
1:24 PM

Dark Light

you make me cry tears of relief
you make me wanna sing
you make me wanna sin
you make me wanna write the most beautiful
words
on how you make my skin crawl with passion
you make me invite myself back to life
you make my soul dance
you make my mind shiver and my body too
and you make me feel like the sun shines brighter
even in your darkness
you make the world feel lighter
you make birds sing the words to your tune
you make me happy
and I don't understand how light shines from the
dark
and how sunflowers are beaming
from the tip of my toes up to the crown of my head
you make the future seem blurry
but I see a rainbow even through the steam
even though you may not be the pot of gold it
stems from
what type of freak am I to gain happiness during
this time?
and what type of person hugs a black pit so tightly?
I still see the galaxy in you
I still see the color
I still see the stars in your eyes
You make me feel like me

Late Again

late again...
it's spreading like wild fire down every inch of my
skin
and the hairs on the back of my neck are
standing up against their own will
I'm late again
Everything is wrong and nothing is right
I'm sitting in one spot but I'm spinning
my hands are icicles
if I touch anything, I will break
don't ask me what's wrong
I'm late again
being disturbed by the sound of a feather dropping
to the floor
walking through a city, seeing people's mouth's
move
and hearing nothing but your heart beat
I could've stopped that thought
I could've stopped this feeling
I'm stronger than this
I should be able to extinguish this fire in my chest
I should know why I'm crying
I should know why I want to move so badly but I'm
stuck
and I don't know anything
the light turned red before I could speed up
I'm late again

Count to 10

There's no reason to have anxiety. Anxiety is caused by real problems and fake problems. Even if the problem is real, the reality can be dealt with peacefully with acceptance, honesty, trust in yourself, and breathing. If the problem isn't real, remember anxiety wants you to think it is.

The Pain of it All

maybe it's me and the tragedies I'm battling with
that make me wander and
create scenarios in my mind
is it really an oasis in the sand or am I just seeing
things because I'm dying of thirst?
Loneliness grips my chest so tight that I can't
breathe
and doubt knocks me out any chance it gets
the future looks as clear as when I take my glasses
off
but I'm hopeful
I just hate this feeling in my chest
because I wanna be held
But the only thing holding me is this cold breeze
giving me goose bumps and over-thought fears
I want to lay and fall into someone completely
And the thought of it brings tears
It makes me terrified because people fall into me
and then they fall out
like a revolving door maybe
I want a love that trickles into a bucket
And, over time, becomes full
just don't pour me out

She's the Best

right now, I feel like I need to take myself out to
dinner
I should buy myself flowers for no reason
just to make my day
I should definitely be getting mad at myself
and thinking about it the whole day
but forgive myself once the moon shows
I also should shower myself with compliments
Make her feel like a super star on a
random Tuesday
I should get into fights with myself
I should learn from myself
Teach myself how to love herself and love other
people- sometimes it feels like she forgot how to
balance
I should make myself food when I'm hungry
add a little extra syrup on my pancakes
because I deserve it
I should tell myself I'm sorry
I should feel all the guilt in the world when
I run my body down... with guilt
I should do things I like
I should give myself whatever it is that I'm craving
simply because I want it
sometimes she'll just have to deal with the
consequences later
I should make sure I stay clean- spiritually,
physically, mentally
I should take care of... myself

She's the only person that will let me down
and always let me back up
and I'll hate her and love her
and destroy her and build her up again

For My Twin

I never knew that the sadness in you could bring
me peace
It's not your pain that I'm embracing
I'm coming to terms with the fact that maybe I'm
here for that reason
Maybe your pain is why I'm here
like shea butter with its rock hard pieces
and as soon as you put them in your hand, they
melt
I'm a Woman and the Woman is God on Earth in
human form
Healers, givers, powerful enough to bring a man
with the pride of no other to tears
Why am I here?
I'm here to be the one to take the sorrow
and make you see the light beaming from the
cracks of its mosaic glass
who knew someone else's pain could be my
power?
Emotional beings we are but we have the capacity
to make you see the moon through the clouds
make you feel every single thing you've never felt
before I came to you
coincidence is tricky
the way the world works, I know me and you are
no mistake
like watering a leaning tulip, I want to help you
grow... not from my own doing but with the

assistance that God so lovingly gave me as the
man's rib
I look at you and want you to be your best YOU.
Whatever that looks like
No ONE completes the other and in no way are you
incompetent- the Black Man is a mastermind and
masterpiece in his own creation
I want to be... I need to be your peace
I want to be the one who referees the fights you
have with your demons and reassure you that you
will always win
and I didn't choose to be this. the Universe did.
And it brought me to you.
as much as the imperfections in me tried to be
more powerful than a power far greater than me, I
still resisted my life's intention
Because I am the resin on your skin that will take
care of those blemishes and scars and slashes and
all the defacing the ones before me left
take pride in those wounds because
those are what led me to you
in my own being, finding reason to be needed is a
woman's prized possession
mothers and wives and sisters and daughters
I am infinite
The world never questions why the wind blows
east or why the sun sets so beautifully or why
waves crash so fiercely
it's the way God made things
just like he made me for you

seventeen.

The first time I felt love, it was cookie cutter love. He did this, he did that, and that's just what made me love him. Even though that was unreciprocated love, I still felt it. But when I think about it, it was love like when you first go to the beach in the summer and get your feet wet but there's still plenty of ocean out there for you to explore.

The second time was probably cookie cutter too. But only this time it was reciprocated. Wait, someone I love gets bubbly on the inside just like I do?! Must be magic. He HAS to be the one. Must be. Then Caleb happens and you realize that that love was a soul mate and most soul mates don't ever stay. They just teach you a thing or two.

My first two loves were like steps on a ladder that I'm climbing in this life. They were only there to get me to somewhere else. But when you get older... and you've been through things... and love seems like a myth to you... when you finally feel it again, you think it's imaginary.

Like, this is another figment of my imagination... but the butterflies in your stomach tell you otherwise. Actually, forget the butterflies. I feel like real love you can't really see clearly sometimes. I say real love you can't see at times because it doesn't always look like unicorns and rainbows.

Sometimes real love looks cloudy. Sometimes it's you getting upset and him still staying. Maybe it's the fact that you always go back and forth. Have fall outs but always fall back in, without losing the sparkle in each other's eyes. It looks like somebody being afraid to open that door again without even knowing your next love is the one with the master key.

Real love is fighting. Real love is thunder clouds and muddy roads and not always pretty. Love and REAL love is only up to the Universe. It will be confusing because it won't look like love. Or it won't look like the love you're "used to". Which will make you question if you ever really knew the four letter word in the first place.

I believe the Universe conspires for each and every one of us to know and learn different types of love at the exact time we need to see them. But the main goal is to ultimately find the soul mate that stays.

7/19/17
10:31 PM

Foreshadow

I'm sitting at my desk at work and I just had a daydream. And I saw myself sitting on a stage at a book fair event of some kind. For my own book. And I just randomly thought of the number 13 as my book title. And the audience, which was pretty big, asked me so many thought provoking questions. Some that I've never even asked myself. But it gave me the most exhilarating feeling- me in the daydream and me presently. Then, after having the time of my life discussing the book, I asked the audience if they wanted to meet Caleb since he was so well known in my life obviously and from the book. I can't tell who brought him out to me and Caleb's face was blurry but he was older but not too much older than he is now. He had an outfit on that was like his 1st birthday but of course, bigger now. I was so happy to be where I was and I had that feeling because of hard work paying off. I could feel it as I sat there.

It's no coincidence that this daydream was only a few seconds long but so detailed. I don't even care if this doesn't happen this way. This was just my sign that it's time. Chelsey, write your book.

8/28/17
1:24 PM

seventeen.

Sometimes I can come off as cold. But I hope each and every one of you understand why at least a little bit now. I'm actually very warm and that's what people feel from me most of the time. But the experiences of life have taken some of my innocence, as many of you may relate to. I'm a thinker. An over thinker. I'm a very connected person to my thoughts and the things around me. But overall, I am the lover of all lovers. I thrive on love and everything about it. In this world, it may feel like a weakness but I know it is my super power. If there is anything I want you to take away from this book, it is that there will be many beginnings and many endings in your life. Take them with a grain of salt. Life is an English class- everything symbolizes something, things happen in life for reasons we may not understand instantly, and if you see no light at the end of the tunnel you're walking, light it yourself. You always write your own story. Don't let anybody steal from you whatever it is that makes you who you are. It takes practice to stay centered and not let toxic energy invade the force field you try so hard to keep around you at all times. Be happy no matter what. I'm still learning and I will always be learning. That's the beauty of life.

Writing this book has taken me back through all the emotions I've felt while writing each passage. But now I see the foreshadowing in it all. The beauty in the pain. And I'm grateful for it. I've loved, I've ached, I've smiled, cried, and I'm still here. With all the beautiful scars to show for it.

Wherever this book takes your heart, try to explore those places. Good, bad, pretty, or ugly. Let's learn about ourselves. Sharing this with you has taught me a lot about myself as well. Thank you for reading- CJM.

39705910R00060

Made in the USA
Middletown, DE
23 March 2019